WE SHALL SERVE YOU NO MORE

By **Dode Sescri**

WORDS TO ELATE

Nineth Agenda

<u>*Disclaimer*</u>

All readers are welcome to challenge the contents of this book, and should examine it with their uttermost intellectual capabilities before they can accept them for reference purposes because they are largely a work of the author's own imaginations.

Some stories given as examples in this book do not represent Factual or historical events but have been used fictitiously to bring out the literal aspects of discussions and also demonstrate the author's intended thoughts and ideas exemplarily. Do not take them too seriously.

This book is stacked up with numerous mini chapters the author refers to as servitudes. Each servitude stands for each idea or topic of discussion.
You will also find some non-English words, the author has used them only for the sake of enhancing description. They are not a result of typo.

Contents

Contention

When I read stories about slavery my heart is torn apart,
the stories are so painful and unbearable that the books
themselves become unreadable, but slavery wasn't like
that before, in the most ancient of nations slavery was a
common practice, in fact you'll learn that slaves were
regarded as part of the owner's family who often cared
for them as they did to their own relatives, when a child is
born into a family of servants then he/she is regarded as a
slave and the family in charge of them becomes the
master. Some people who were living under a good
master had better lives than those who were not slaves.
I have come across some ancient texts that revealed
some good relationships between the slaves and their
masters, who had a strong bond and lived by simple rules,
there was a very thin line between the word servant and a
slave, a servant works for a pay, and goes home to feed
their families with the little pay they have gained, a slave
on the other hand had nowhere to go, and therefore
works for the masters family without any pay, but then all
his needs and those of his children are taken care of by
the owner, slave families lived across the street just near
the owners home, when you are dirt poor and famine has
struck the country hard, better be some rich fellows slave
than to perish, an owner of many slaves has less food for
himself because he has more mouths to feed, if a slave
wanders off into the desert he/she will perish, there is no
life in the wilderness, better stay in the masters house
and get plenty of food and water to drink than to die out

in the desert, all you need to do is help in taking care of their flock and their other property, many good owners would fiercely defend their slaves from abuse and exploitation from others even members of their own family. Like the slaves and servants of the great kings of Timbuktu and the Sultans of Zanzibar, all treated their servants and slaves with nobility.

But when it comes to the transatlantic slave trade it's a different story, a platoon of pirates swarmed across the seas, and travelled from ocean to ocean carrying humans like cargo, the large-scale exploitation of others made it impossible to treat them with the least amount of care, they were then sold off to cruel farmers, abusive owners…… and the stories of cruelty goes on.
Many of these slave traders were pagans and came from heathen nations, and have never comprehended how to treat a fellow human being, it is no wonder some of the experiences of these slaves were so vile that many people prefer not to raise those issues once again, they better remain as bad memories of the past. Nobody wants to talk about it anymore. It came to our thoughts that people from the global north had no knowledge of what it's like to be a slave yourself, none ever pitied them.

If people come across an article about slavery, they instantly become curious about it, some will figure it out to be the sad transatlantic slave trade of the last few centuries, so they quickly toss it aside, no one wants to read something that will cause them pain or heartbreak, slavery should be a none-issue in this twenty first century as for everyone else' knowledge.

Every researcher in this field aspires to become a master motivational speaker someday. If you want to talk about slavery then better be cautious with your choice of words, if you bring up stories of masters who were cruel to their slaves then also remember that there were those who were very kind to them and treated them like a family, so as not to become too biased and annoy your keen listeners.

Servitude-1-The earliest Forms of slavery

Civilizations have always depended on slavery to advance their development programs. All the great civilizations of the Past, all of them from Sumerian, Assyrian, Babylonian, Persian, Greek and Roman all had established institutions of slavery to survive. Even ancient Egyptian cities were full of slaves. Most of Egyptian aristocracy owned slaves, even an average family could buy slaves to help on their homes and farms as long as they could afford them. There is a lot of Egyptian hieroglyphs talking about slaves and slavery in general.

In ancient past, whenever cities or countries went to war, the loser would be forced to hand over his material possessions such as cutlery made of precious metals, if the inhabitants of a city are defeated to the point where there are no male survivors with the ability to carry arms, their grain would be looted as well. All their artifacts of gold, silver, bronze, fine linen fabrics and almost every valuable items in their homes would be looted and carried off to the victor's homes. If there are any survivors after the battle, they would be carried off as slaves as well to the enemy's territory where they will spend their entire lives in servitude. Slaves were always spoils of war in the past and the slave owner had the power of life and death over his slaves, he did with them as he pleased.

Some Greek City States had so many slaves that they would outnumber the Greek citizens themselves by a ratio of three to one. However numerous they were, they were pressed down so hard they could not bring themselves to rise up against their overlords. Then Rome was also another empire that greatly depended on its institutions of slavery to survive, almost everything in the Roman way of life needed slaves to function well. The romans were infamous for their cruelty. For the roman society to continue to function, they had to continue conquering more land and enslave its people in order to fill in the coffers of the empire, in the last few centuries of the empire the Romans realized how unsustainable their way of life was, they ran out of new land and peoples to conquer and enslave. The rebellion of a single barbarian tribe could risk destabilizing the entire empire.

There is mention of slavery in many religious books, some bible texts written thousands of years ago teaches people how to treat slaves and reminds man that there is a higher power that will eventually judge them for the way they live with people that serve them. The Israelites were slaves to the Egyptians for many generations before God sent prophet Moses to deliver them from their suffering. As the story goes, the Egyptian pharaoh of the time stubbornly refused to let them go which in turn invited God's wrath upon the Egyptians. As the Jewish account states, this experience was so humiliating for the Egyptian pharaohs that they forbade any record of the event, only neighboring kingdoms like Hittites and Moabites recorded Israelis exodus from Egypt.

Slavery at the time was a matter of convenience and opportunity, if you defeat another nations' troops in battle then their women and children automatically became your slaves. However, cruel it may appear to us today, this was the culture at the time. Slavery of the ancients had nothing to do with race or religion. It was all about taking advantage of your weakest neighbors. The strongest fellow in the neighborhood makes all the surrounding neighbors his servants.

Servitude-2-The Economy of the Modern World is still Based On some form of Slavery

Only a few countries have overcome the trenches brought forth by modern slavery, countries like China have pulled their citizens out of poverty despite the odds being stacked against them for decades. Honestly speaking, the Chinese worked their asses off to lift themselves out of poverty. Even though I am not a Chinese myself I give the Chinese people a thumbs up for believing in themselves and staying committed to their work, it was a long painful journey yet they continued to struggle on, they are almost there at the summit right now, hard work and determination is a virtue highly praised in many Asian countries that often brings out the good in people in the society, countries like Japan, South Korea and Singapore became known as Asian tigers after they got their people out of poverty. And there are other Asian tigers already on their way to prosperity, we are seeing these countries like Indonesia, Thailand and Vietnam coming up really fast and they are almost catching up with the big boys. Asian tiger nations became rich in just a few years even when they had very little natural resources, all this happened because of their sheer determination and hard work.

This prosperity wasn't that easy, it came at a huge price, especially to countries like China. Well, this is a story we all know, after decades of desperation created by Chairman Mao's polices, the Chinese decided to experiment with capitalism which resulted in their country blossoming in just a few decades. With the influx of money from foreign firms, the Chinese authorities had no choice but to send hundreds of millions of people into factories to generate enough revenue for the local government. Even though they were paid just peanuts, they refused to give up and dutifully completed their work without complaints. The Chinese are a hardy folk, commitment to one's work is deeply rooted into Chinese culture and will happily do any job assigned to them.

The new form of work brought many benefits as well as drawbacks. First of all, let's talk about the exploitation of the workers in the factories owned by foreign companies, Chinese workers are forced to work extremely long hours with very little pay in a very dangerous environment. This has led to millions of workers dying from exhaustion from overwork. They became the unfortunate statistics of our modern world. Tens of millions more perished from the environmental pollution created by these foreign factories. When China instantly became the factory of the world, every other major industry tried to put up a factory in that nation, their cheap labor and ease of doing business was unmatchable anywhere else in the world. Entire manufacturing plants & factories were uprooted from the rich developed nations of the world and then replanted in China, they still would have received more things to produce had it not been for the pandemic, when covid hit in 2020 and disrupted the supply chains, industries started to have second thoughts about relying on one country for their entire production capacity. They had no choice but to start diversifying.

Other than manufacturing of cool tech gadgets, another industry that has been grabbing headlines lately has been the fashion industry. Outsourcing of garment productions by the big boys in the fashion industry has been exposed by some pretty brutal accidents in developing Asian countries, a few years ago, the world awoke to the shock of seeing entire buildings collapse onto workers, these turned out to be poorly constructed multi storey buildings hosting thousands of garments workers. The factory owners were gullible businessmen who traded workers safety for profits. Some buildings were so poorly constructed that they collapsed just months after construction was finished, others had almost zero safety measures like having simple fire extinguishers in the building.

You know the garment industry is very vulnerable to fires, and when the flames began to make their move, entire buildings were consumed in just a matter of minutes trapping in hundreds of people. The buildings were overly congested with so many people that there was hardly any oxygen to breathe. The ***Bangladeshi garment factory disasters*** opened the eyes of the world to the really dark side of Outsourcing, big fashion brands outsourced their garments to another company who would produce them much more cheaply, and that company then outsources it to yet another company to produce the clothes at a much lower cost. The supply chain then becomes so long that you never know who is doing what. A perfect recipe for disaster. And when fires start consuming thousands of workers or building collapsing on them, the big fashion brands want to be no part of it, the reason they outsource their production to these developing countries with very little regulation is to distance themselves from those factories when disaster strikes. It looks like everybody is cutting corners in the industry, everybody wants quick easy money without thinking about the consequences.

We really enjoy shopping for cheap products at our local malls yet we never stop to think for once where those products are made. What kinds of hardships the workers go through, and the environmental impacts of that production. After the Bangladeshi Garment Factory incidences, I went straight into my closet to check on my clothes, I looked at the tags, I was shocked to discover that nearly two thirds of all the clothes in my wardrobe had the tag, *"Made in Bangladesh"*. I was shocked to discover that most of my trousers, shirts, t-shirts, jumpers, and coats were all made in Bangladesh. I then reflected on the images of the workers being pulled out of rubble of collapsed factory buildings, some were as young as twelve years, "Oh my God! These are children who should be in school, yet they were locked up in factories to make clothes for guys in some rich countries." It saddens my heart to think that some of the clothes I am wearing today could have been made by children who missed a chance to go to school or enjoy their childhood. It's such a cruel world we live in today.

I was really heartbroken to see those images of charred bodies of poor people whose only crime was trying to support their families. They never tried to rob or hurt anyone, they rose up in the morning one day and went to work just like everybody else, not knowing that it was going to be their last journey. We have seen & heard critics blaming the Bangladeshi government for not putting up stricter regulations to protect its citizens from exploitation, well that is easier said than done. The garment industry makes a significant proportion of the country's GDP, if the government starts the crackdown right now, it could destabilize the economy, it is a very risky and delicate part of the economy and are therefore obliged to proceed with caution. Rich foreign companies are aware of this destitute nature of many Bangladeshi youth, they waste no time in exploiting their citizens and extracting as much labor resource as they could. Should the Bangladeshi government decide to shut down the entire garment industry, the big boys of the fashion world would simply monkey branch to another country, they will easily find another developing country with high unemployment rate to exploit. When factories get shut down in one country they immediately pop up in another part of the word. It's a never-ending vicious cycle.

Over three quarters of the world's population live from hand to mouth, paycheck to paycheck, most folks don't even have a single dime in their savings bank account, so that even when the work stops even for a week, it puts the workers and their families in Grave economic crisis. If a local factory suddenly shuts down, it puts all the people in that town in grave danger as they do not have alternative reliable means of generating income other than working at the factory floor itself.

Or when a manual laborer gets involved in a non-occupational accident, the hospital bills alone consume all the little spare cash they had left, which eventually leaves their dependent children distraught, homelessness is such a high risk such that it takes only a few weeks of dried-up salaries for someone and their family to get thrown out of their house. It takes only a few dozen days of unemployment for the risk of starvation to manifest in the family home. This is tantamount to modern day slavery.

Even though we live in a highly technologically advanced society today, nothing about work has changed, it's still demanding and backbreaking as it were thousands of years ago. At the dawn of industrial revolution, people thought that technology will reduce the workload on humanity as machines will take over the most difficult time-consuming tasks while people take their daywork time off to rest, it in fact did the exact opposite, people were working harder and longer than ever despite the new technology that had been brought in by inventors and scientists.

Servitude-3-Slavery In Arabia

Slavery In Arabia has existed for millennia, it was a common practice long before the pre-Islamic era began, the Arabs did not invent slavery, they only made it more efficient, the practice itself is many thousands of years older than any Islamic civilization. the caliphate only institutionalized the practice and made it a part of state proper functioning organ, there are still several states in the Arab world where slavery is still practiced, this includes Mauritania in North Africa and Yemen in the Gulf. The practice of slavery has been outlawed in Arabia, they have only driven it underground. The problem is that this culture has existed for so long that it's hard to force communities to stop it, it has been there for millennia, their parents, grandparents and all their ancestors either owned slaves or were slaves themselves. Slavery in Arabia however was different from what we have seen in the trans-Atlantic slave trade.

There are cases like in Mauritania where slaves were freed by human rights activists only to return to their former masters just a few weeks after being freed. This was because life of slavery was the only thing they had known all their lives. In fact, they didn't see it as any kind of oppression, they saw their owners as generous nobles who allowed them to live in their own homes in exchange for doing light household chores. They went back to their slave masters and asked for forgiveness for running away from them.

Arabs are known to be some of the most hospitable people in the world, it is well known fact that Arab culture encourages them to be friendly towards one another and even towards strangers, for centuries, it has been a well-known Arab culture to welcome travelers into their homes, give them warm meal and a nice place to sleep until they find strength to continue on with their journey the following day. This culture has continued for such a long time, it existed even in pre-Islamic Arabia. Arabs in general are very welcoming and friendly people. Much of those good traditions are quickly deteriorating in the modern world because of a rise in violent crime and terrorism. As the saying goes, courtesy has its limits. You can be generous to a person but not too generous to the point where you forget about your own personal safety and that of your family.

Just like people on other continents, Arabs also like flaunting their wealth, they are however not mean or selfish as people in other parts of the world. The oil rich gulf states like to share their newly found wealth with their neighbors and strangers that may want to work for them. We have seen how the populations of some gulf nations like UAE are composed mostly of non-citizens, expatriates and immigrants from all over the world live and work in the UAE, Qatar, Oman, Bahrain and Saudi Arabia.

The Oil Boom in the middle east in the last few decades has allowed many gulf nations to become incredibly rich, they have used the oil money to modernize their national infrastructure, their economies have mushroomed at an incredibly fast pace. Megacities have sprung up all over the place, attracting skilled and unskilled workers from all over the world. It's this influx of migrant workers that has allowed their previously small cities to be quickly turned into glittering metropolises. In gulf cities like Doha and Dubai, the immigrants from rich western countries have named themselves ***"expatriates"***, a fancy term they used to distinguish themselves from the immigrants from other continents like Africa and Asia.

They claim that people from these poor parts of the world should be called immigrants because they are employed in the unskilled labor market. A lot of folks from Africa and Asia are the ones working in the construction industry, toiling away in the searing heat of the middle east to build those shining buildings you see in their cities. They are the ones also employed in the households working as domestic servants. Human rights activists have accused the gulf boom of fueling some form of modern-day slavery, they accuse gulf countries of allowing the exploitation of manual laborers by construction companies, they have very long workings hours, they spend the whole day outside on construction sites, enduring the extremely hot Arabian sun, often for very little pay. Many of them work for companies that have poor safety records and lots of them have unfortunately lost their lives as a direct result of hazardous work environments. The gulf nations however have come out with their own statists to debunk this biased myth, saying that most of the immigrants lost their lives in other areas that are not directly related to their work, this includes road accidents and other unrelated illnesses they picked up elsewhere outside the gulf.

Another issue that came up for the migrant workers is their horrendous living conditions, to save the little money they earn from their work, manual laborers have been forced to live in congested hostels where they often face security and hygiene issues. You find about eight to ten men sharing a tiny little room that was meant to be used by only two people. They all find this kind of lifestyle appalling, but what choice do they have? There is absolutely no privacy in these hostels. Just a few years ago, photos started doing rounds on social media under the label, *"Other Parts of Doha & Dubai you never get to see"*. Some of the workers took selfies of their miserable lives in their hostels and sent them to their families back at home using social media. Some for them were really complaining about their work, they claimed the money being paid to them is not the amount they had been promised earlier when they were still in their home countries. They said they had been lied to by their employing companies, they got only a fraction of what they were told they would receive in compensation. Since the workers are bound to their employers by the **Kafala system**, they cannot independently switch their jobs to a more suitable one so they remain stuck in those countries until when their contract is over. Their employers have complete control over them, they cannot change work or travel out of the country without their Sponsor's permission.

the tiny gulf nation of Qatar has made history for being the first Arab country to host the FIFA world cup, this has given them an appointment to make the event as bright and colorful as possible. Since the announcement by FIFA in 2010, Qatar has embarked on a nationwide construction program, they are pouring money into massive projects like streets, roads, hotels, and stadiums, and guess who is building those shining stadiums? Yes, you got it right, the immigrants from other developing countries. Qatari state has been accused by human rights activists of turning a blind eye on the horrendous workers exploitation that is going on in their country. At some point they were even calling for the boycotting of the FIFA 2022 world cup until the Qatar state properly addresses the issues of migrant workers abuse. The Qatari state on the other hand denies any complicity in supporting such behavior and said they would take proper legal action against construction companies that exploit or abuse any of its workers. This has continued to be a game of cat and mouse ever since.

Servitude-4-The Endless Plight of Domestic Workers Around the Gulf

Day in Day out we hear horror stories of Domestic workers who have been to the middle east, they are mostly from poor countries in South east Asia and Africa. Unlike many countries in the world, the gulf and many Arab nations have their own sets of rules, many of them still harbor medieval perceptions where they see domestic workers as their slaves. In many Arab cultures anyone who works for you for such a long time as an indentured servant is of course your slave. Thanks to the **Kafala system**, the employers have complete control over their employees' lives, they sponsored everything about them, all from their countries of origin, apart from the work fees they gave away, they also paid for their travel expenses. This sponsorship programs means the employer has complete control over their workers. They take their passports which forces them to stay in the employer's home until the contract is over.

These women are also made vulnerable to abuse by their employers. A vast majority of them fall into the hands of good Arabs who treat them well as if they are members of their own family, but there is a small proportion who unfortunately land into the hands of some really nasty bosses. That Arab family home becomes a place of torment for some of these ladies, many of them are shocked by the extent of the work they have to do in those homes. According to the testimony of some girls that have returned to their home countries, they say that they never have any rest, they claimed to have experienced up to twenty hours a day of backbreaking work. Sometimes with only two to three hours of sleep per working day.

From scrubbing the floors, doing the laundry, cooking and doing dishes, cleaning the children, taking them to school and checking on them every minute they are at home, it's such an horrific experience for some women who go there very ill prepared. They get traumatized in the first few weeks when the harsh reality of their work hits them. Returnees say that whenever they asked for a minute of rest, their female bosses would reply, " didn't you come here for work, this is the work you were so desperate to get that you had to leave your home country, now get back to work!" they spend their entire days doing backbreaking work while being constantly yelled at, to them there is nothing you ever seem to do right. They call them derogative terms like "**Khadima**" or "**eabd**" and for the domestic workers who understand Arabic, these are vilifying terms that are used to refer to slaves. Some of these returnees claim that a lot of Arab women are so lazy that they don't have time for even their own children.

They leave everything to the domestic servant and sit on the armchair all day doing nothing but just gossiping with their friends.

In east Africa people continue to travel to the gulf to do domestic work despite the plethora of horror stories on social media of women who have been to the place. There has been an increasing culture of families calling for community prayers to be held for the sake of their children before sending them off to the gulf. *"Oh God please watch over our daughter as she travels over to work in Arabia,"* they ask the heavens in desperation, they have no choice but to send off their daughters to the unknown. They hold their breadths as they watch their baby daughters board those planes knowing at the back of their heads that it may be their last journey alive. Bodies arrive into east African regions weekly, of women who went over to look for greener pastures in the middle east, only to return in coffins. It's such a sad fate indeed. No one is saying that all Arabs are bad people, but it's the distraught cases of those few women that have returned in body bags that have sent shock waves across the region.

Domestic workers have almost zero rights in the middle east. The boss can treat their employees as they please. These go to work in homes that are full of people, there are reported cases where they have no privacy at all, the rooms they sleep in either have no properly functioning locks or doors. So their employer can just bump into their rooms at any time they please. Sometimes they have no rooms at all, they are forced to sleep in the living room or the stores where grain or cleaning items are kept.

There are hidden cameras watching them everywhere they go including the very bathrooms they are using. There are stories on social media where domestic workers said they were shocked to discover that their employer had been watching them closely every time they took a shower. They report these incidences to the agents who unfortunately have no power to enforce anything. The homes are full of men both members of the family and relatives who sometimes make inappropriate advances on these girls, sometimes the man of the house puts so much pressure on the maid using threats to force the lady to sleep with him, and when the lady of the house catches the domestic servant in bed with her husband, she goes ballistic, she is enraged beyond belief, that the lowly servant she had brought into her home is now trying to steal her husband. Even if the girl says that it's the man that initiated the wicked act, no one would believe her, the lady of the house has no reason to believe otherwise. She retaliates by either poisoning her or beating her to death. Such cases are so common that every domestic worker that goes to the gulf is advised to reject any kind of sexual advances of any man in that home because If the lady of the house finds out about the heinous act, she will definitely show no mercy.

Critics say that the gulf domestic workers rights are so bad that sometimes girls who ran away from the homes they were working in for being violated get absolutely no help, when they reported to the police, they ended up being violated themselves by the very same police they went to seek protection from. They got locked up and accused of adultery when they should have been treated as victims of sexual violence.

On the positive side however, there are domestic workers who have praised the gulf nations for their generosity, even though Arab countries are not the richest in the world, they have shared a lot of their wealth with others that are less fortunate than themselves. They try to treat their workers nicely and pay them well, just like everyone else they too are religious folks and believe that God will judge anyone that treats their servants with cruelty. Arabs are more generous than the average human. There are many continents in the world that are much richer than gulf nations yet they haven't allowed workers from other parts of the world to get a small share of their country's economy like the gulf nations have done, they are welcoming to everyone that wishes to work and live in their countries, not unless you are an extremely dangerous criminal, they welcome everyone with open arms. A huge percentage of the population of many gulf countries is made up of foreign-born residents from many parts of the world. This itself should be a testament of how generous and welcoming Arabia is compared to some filthy rich countries in other parts of the world like in Asia, north America, or western Europe. The world should give the gulf states a thumbs up for providing employment opportunities for many people, some of whom are not even their fellow Arabs.

Servitude-5-Idi Amin's Revenge

Idi Amin Dada the former president of Uganda is probably one of the most misunderstood heads of state that that has ever run an African country. His presidency is associated with incredible brutality towards the citizens of the country he ruled called Uganda, there is a lot of things said about Amin that was true but there was a lot more that was nothing but grim tales created by his haters. Although many Ugandans remember him for his reign of terror that lasted for nearly a decade, there are things he did that made some Africans to like him.

With his little knowledge and understanding of the world, he tried to do away with the old institutions of slavery put in place by European colonialism, he said things that angered his former masters, the British, he hurled very vulgar words at the British monarch.

Anyone can be quick to judge this flamboyant man, but when you look at his life history, this is a man that had a very rough childhood. He grew up during the rough times of British occupation, during the last few decades of British rule of the country, he served his country *(British masters)* well, and despite his little education he rose in the ranks of the military because of his bravery and ability to bring swift victory to battlefields. He was even used by the British to help quench rebellion in a neighboring colony called Kenya, the rebellion by then called the *Mau*

Mau rebellion instigated by the local Kikuyu tribe was getting out of control and the British had to bring in reinforcements from the UK as well as the neighboring colonies. Idi Amin happened to be one of the troops and he did an excellent job, he fought hard and won, back at his home in Uganda he was rewarded a promotion to a relatively high military office in the country. He slowly rose through ranks before he later became president. During his time in the military Amin saw how the colonial powers used the locals against one another, the troops nicknames *"Kings African Rifles"* were majorly troops picked from the local communities and trained by the colonial army to serve the British Crown's interests, British hardly ever did the policing themselves, whenever there were rebellions they would send these African troops to discipline the locals, there were a lot of documented brutal beatings by these troops and sometimes responsible for homicides, the locals weren't happy to see their own sons being used against them by an occupying foreign power. Some troops were appalled by many of their actions, especially when they are being asked to drive off local communities from their land to make way for white farmers. Amin promised to make a difference should he get a position of authority and Power.

He kept some of his promises when he got into presidential office, one of the first things he did was to Send all foreigners packing to their so-called places of origin. Even though Uganda was relatively prosperous at the time, he was disappointed to see very few indigenous

Ugandans in the management roles of the big companies in his country, most businesses at the time were owned by Ugandans who were of either European or Asian origins, even though some of them had stayed in the country for decades he still saw them as invading foreigners who had been fleecing the country of its natural resources, when he saw that the jobs available for the indigenous Ugandans was only carrying heavy luggage for the rich European or Asian guys, he was heartbroken, even though they did incredibly hard work they were paid very little and therefore had very little chance of climbing the economic ladder. This is when he gets the idea that by sending off all those filthy rich children of colonialists, indigenous Ugandans will finally have a chance to prosper and improve their lives for real.

Even though he didn't have the knowledge to make him think about how disastrous his actions could turn out to be, he was acting purely from instincts, he wholeheartedly wanted to put an end to the institutions of slavery and subjugation he had lived through since childhood.

Another thing that hurt Amin's feelings was the way he saw the colonialists being treated like royalty while the locals languished in poverty, some European folks who had high ranks in the military at times refused to walk on foot and forced the locals to carry them on their shoulders. This was unimaginable in many parts of Africa. Most tribes didn't carry their own chieftains' thrones on their backs. As long as they were perfectly healthy, they were just fine walking alongside everyone else. But here comes some crazy general who thinks himself as deity and enjoys wiping his feet using the garments of others that he believes are inferior to him. It was this inferiority perceptions that was a clashing point between many Africans and the Europeans. They were treated nicely by their own indigenous leaders prior to the arrival of the colonialists, but when the Europeans came along, they were treated no better than wild animals.

When Idi Amin went into office after his coup, he forced British guys to carry his sofa on their backs, just like he was forced to carry colonial generals when he was a low-ranking military officer. the British papers ridiculed him extensively for this, but for him he saw it as a payback for many decades of subjection, he wanted the British to feel exactly how he felt like when its they that are placed at the bottom of the social hierarchy. These images caused him to be ridiculed by many especially the Europeans, on the flipside many Africans praised him for his actions, there were many African leaders who felt exactly as he did but could not bring themselves to the point of publicly expressing their emotions because of fear of backlash form their former colonial masters.
Amin gave himself extravagant titles such as... **Conqueror of the British empire** & **The Last King of Scotland**.. All this was an attempt to forget the subjugation he went through in his youth

Servitude-6-Slavery in the Americas

We can confidently say that there are elements of racism still present in North America but we cannot say that the US is the most racist country in the world, just because the Yankees have been exposed by modern day technology doesn't mean that they are the worst of the Worst Folks in the World, it's just that some ugly skeletons in America's closet have been exposed in the eyes of the whole world. European colonialism took its toll on the people of south America just as it did to the people of North America. In central and Latin America there was a continent wide subjugation of the indigenous peoples by the invading Spanish conquistadors, who took over most of their valuable land and property, the fertile fields were seized by the invaders and indigenous people driven out of their land to make way for European settlers, who then forced some of those indigenous folks to work on the farms for little to no pay, the very land that once belonged to the indigenous folks now is in the hands of the European settlers who are now striving to exploit it as much as they can. Any land that had minerals such as gold, silver and other precious metals was exploited to the fullest, indigenous people were forced to work on the mines. When there was a shortage of labor as result of mass deaths of the indigenous folks because of poor working conditions as well as the deadly diseases brought about by the Europeans, the Colonizers sorted labor from elsewhere, they shipped in millions of people from the African continent to do the hard work in the Americas that the Europeans themselves weren't willing to do. Let's touch a few countries in central and South

America that suffered immensely as a result colonial as well as trans-Atlantic slave trade.

1.Bolivia.

There is an infamous story in the modern-day state of Bolivia of How the Spanish conquistadors exploited their country for many centuries and ended up destroying the environment as well as the lives of the local indigenous Peoples. Back then it was just another Spanish colonial outpost. Millions or people are said to have perished over the centuries while working on the **Cerro Rico de Potosí** located in the Andes Mountain region of Bolivia. This region alone was responsible for producing more than a half of the world's silver at the time, the workers had no rights of any kind, and their frequent deaths therefore went unexamined.

I try to imagine millions of people losing their lives at a single mine, how many more died in the whole of central and south America put together? The negative experiences of this kind of exploitations are still very fresh in the minds of the Bolivian People today, nearly every Bolivian has a loved one or knows someone that perished at the *Cerro Rico.* The Bolivians are now very weary of foreign companies coming into their country to exploit their natural resources and local people while giving nothing in return.

A couple of years back the Bolivian government blocked some foreign mining companies because of their refusal to comply with the new tighter regulation that had been put into place. The new rules had been drafted by the state to protect the economy and its People from overexploitation. The Bolivian people still have fresh memories of what the Spanish did to their silver, they didn't want the same happening now over the New Gold Rush. Lithium is the most valuable mineral for the electronic technologies of the world today and Bolivia has a significant share of the world's deposits, the nation therefore wants to make the most of it. Many Bolivians and experts in other South American countries believe that the removal of President Evo Morales from office in 2019 had something to do with his strict policies towards minerals & mining, he had become too overprotective over his country's natural resources and therefore had to be removed to make way for Big Business, they say that the removal of Morales from office was a deliberate coup against a leader who may have been just trying to protect his own people. Morales and his aides didn't want a repeat of the silver loot by the Spanish over centuries ago. Another sad story of slavery in history is trying to repeat itself.

2.Brazil

Brazil holds the crown of south America in terms of the nation's total landmass and population size. It's the biggest of the big boys in Latin America, It also hosts the greatest biodiversity of flora and Fauna on the continent. They are rich in all kinds of mineral wealth, something that has been exploited for generations by the advanced economies of the world. Due to the demands of land for agriculture and mining the world-famous amazon rainforest has been exploited so much that only a tiny proportion of its original size remains, its now a ghost of its former self.

Brazil is also home to the largest populations of Afro Latinos, nearly half of its two hundred million plus people ethnically identify as black or have some form of African ancestry, they are descendants of African slaves that were brought into the country to help on the plantations. Since then, afro Brazilians have lived in the country for centuries. The systems of slavery that brought them into the country however have not changed that much, most afro Brazilians live in abject poverty, they are associated with the life in the *ghettos* locally known as *favelas*, of the thousands of people killed every year by the Brazilian Police more than three quarters of them are always young black men, that's way more than statistics is in the USA.

Despite nearly half of the Population of the country having some drop of African blood in them, there is very little representation of this colored community in nearly every important aspect of the society, they have very little representation in the government, business world and the media. There are no black billionaires in Brazil, most of the wealthiest entrepreneurs are all white. They have been completely erased by the media, its like they do not exist. In the media and entertainment industry, you never see them as news anchors or reporters, in fact Brazil presented its first black news anchor in 2018, which was received by the world as an historic achievement many decades after the media industry flourished in the country, the Brazilian media likes showing afro Brazilians only when there is something bad happening in the *favelas*, that's the time when the cameras suit them appropriately, the only place you would find them is in football fields and the carnivals, because all these professions require extreme talent which can only be found in the favelas. The greatest footballer of all time is a Brazilian named Pele, who happens to be an Afro Brazilian, he too just like other sports stars rose from the favelas, the tough life in there hardened him so well that he easily conquered the world with his three world cups, that is a record that no other footballer has ever achieved to this very date, ***"three world cup tittles?"*** that is insane man. The story of Pele is a testament that afro Brazilians can never make it in life through conventional methods like borrowing money from a bank & investing it to grow their businesses, Pele's only way out of poverty was through track and field and he was successful in that. Just like in America, the only way most black men can get out of poverty is through sports and athletics, no bank ever wants to lend them a dime to start a business.

Many experts argue that racism is way worse in other countries like Brazil than it is in the US. Which may be a pill too hard to swallow for some Brazilians. When you travel to Rio carnivals you are blown away by the beauty of the party, the joy of the participants as well as stadium fans, it's something you can never forget, you then leave the country thinking, 'what a happy city to live in, its partying all the time, I should probably move here for good." little do visitors know that the Brazilian society is only united when either Playing Soccer or Dancing to samba music, soccer and samba are events that enable Brazilians to momentarily forget the negative impacts that slavery has left in their country.

3.Argentina

Last but not the least on our menu here is another large south American country, Argentina just like all other Latin American countries is also a product of colonialism and slavery, the conquistadors did the loot and plunder that they are usually accustomed to and left the nation in the modern state it is right now, but the institutions of colonialism and slavery that built the nation are still present to the current date.

What baffles people the most is when they travel to many Latin American countries like Colombia, Venezuela, Bolivia, Brazil and Peru, it's easy to come across an indigenous person when walking along the streets of its major cities. But such a thing can never be said about Argentina, you can walk across streets of Argentine cities for days and never come across an indigenous person, critics often say that *there are indigenous people in all of Latin America except Argentina, only God knows what the Spaniards did to the indigenous folk*. The same can be said about black folks, millions of them were shipped there centuries ago to help in manual labor, but none of their trace seems to ever remain of them, it looks like a short while ago they all vanished into thin air like mist, never to be seen again.

4.Caribbean

The Caribbean Nations Like Jamaica, Haiti and Dominican Republics were the centers of sugar production for the British empire, even to the late fifties the British royal family still owned slave farms in the Caribbean.
Even to this day, there are still remnants of the colonial past scattered all over the island. The modern-day citizens of the Caribbean who are direct descendants of those slaves brought onto the continent centuries ago peacefully dwell on the island. They have kept records of their parents' oral traditions that were passed down from one generation to the next.
When the Queen Elizabeth visited Jamaica in 1957. she was welcomed by many with open arms but there are those who didn't really feel happy about her presences since she still owned some slave land in the area, even centuries after abolition of slavery by the British Parliament, there was still traces of slavery in the former British empire.

The Behavior of the British Queen in the Last Decades also caused a lot of outrage around the world as it reminded the People the long-gone negative impacts of slavery. The queen mother has a habit of putting on gloves whenever she is about to shake the hands of leaders in developing countries especially Africa and the Caribbean. African Leaders saw it very clearly that the British queen always puts on her glows whenever she was about to shake the hands of an African leader but removes those same gloves when about to greet a European or north American head of state. This was the pre-pandemic era remember, it even caused some African leaders to avoid visiting Britain to meet with the queen because they may be publicly humiliated when they see the queen putting on her protective gloves before passing greetings.

This kind of behavior is very insulting especially to African leaders, even though they are heads of states in their home countries, with the best health care staff travelling with them, they are still looked down on by Birmingham Palace as if they were diseased rats who have travelled to England and Europe to spread the Bubonic Plague onto European populations. This is just another reason where there Is still great mistrust between The UK and many African governments, behavioral straits that carry a long sad story, if the queen were to put on gloves before greeting ordinary African folks that may be a little bit acceptable, but doing that to heads of state is way too disrespectful.
Princess Diana was one of the few royals to break with old fashioned British traditions and went ahead to embrace ordinary citizens.

The world was amazed when she went into an African hospital, shook the hands of some patients and hugged others, she was informed by the doctors that the illnesses they had could not be spread through shaking hands or hugging, she was berated by the royal family and the entire British government for this action claiming that she was putting herself and her own family in grave danger. Her humility and kindness were the things that made the world fall in love with her. At the time it was unthinkable for a British Monarch to shake the hands of an African leader without wearing protective gloves but Diana went about embracing ordinary folks without wearing a single glove, proving to the society that she truly understood the feelings of the ordinary people. Not everybody is born with a sliver spoon in their mouths, and those in high places can come down to earth and interact with the lowly of the low individuals.

Servitude-7-When BLM Protesters first sang "I can't Breathe"

For those of us that remember, The phrase. "I can't breathe wasn't invented after the killing of George Floyd in 2020, in fact there was an incident that happened some years back when another black man died under similar circumstances. In the month of July in the year 2014, four police officers pounced on an unarmed black man, in the video he appeared to be resisting arrest, half a dozen policemen then wrestle him down, some sitting on his chest and neck, he was heard over the ground there faintly screaming for help, saying, " I can't breathe, I can't breathe, such incidences of unarmed black men dying in the hands of police officers during arrests is not something new to the black community in the US, it's something they go through every other day, every black parent in America lectures their children to be weary of crooked cops, to always comply however brutal the officer may be in his line of duties, they beg their young boys to be submissive even when harassed or wrongfully arrested, this is because they fear that their children may not survive the encounter to return home to them later. "it's better to comply and get arrested for a crime you didn't commit than to struggle and die in the hands of an officer." That would be a burden too much to bear for the parents, they have seen many of their friends perish that way and therefore do really know what they are saying. They are always taught to turn the other cheek.

There are black officers in the law enforcement agencies, who sometimes witness these wrongs happening but they would never speak up because of fear of retribution from their white superiors, those that managed to speak up have ended up being shown the door and got kicked out of the police academies.

The Way the BLM Protesters are putting this story makes it appears as if these are things that have been happening for generations, it only took the help of technology and global attention for these issues to be properly discussed in that country, the cameras didn't capture even a tenth of what is happening out there in the dark corners of America. Be it strangulation or shooting of unarmed suspects, the story always has a similar ending. It's the poor black man meeting a miserable end. Another video emerged in the nineties of a group of white officers who were brutally beating an unarmed black man*(Rodney King)*, the man was laying on the ground trying to protect his head from the blows that were coming at him, the officers used every knowledge they learnt from movie fights, they were punching him, kicking him and beating him with sticks and baseball bats.

Despite the gruesome nature of the incident none of the officers involved got even a single day behind bars or any kind of punishment. There were no suspensions, no firings and no disciplinary actions taken against them, according to the black community the courts were biased when they were let go scot-free, and the police departments they worked for embraced them with opens arms as though they were kids returning home to their parents after a long school day of tiring study.

When the BLM Protesters first entered the streets in 2014, they were relatively few in numbers and belonged to only one particular racial group, they were quickly dismissed by the local authorities as just another group of rowdy youth looking for trouble, even though *Eric Garner's killing* was reported by the mainstream media, it didn't get the steam it needed to cause widespread public outcry, there were even accusations that the first batch of BLM Protesters was a terrorist group that was being funded by the Russians to destabilize America. People said all kinds of horrible things about them, this was a group that got sidelined by the society, it was treated as an outcast, and could not therefore speak for the community they claimed to be fighting for. Fortunately for them, their actions got approved by the society a few years down the line, they got vindicated when they heard the whole world singing to the tunes that they have been trying to drum into the ears of the folks they are protesting against. Thanks to the Covid Lockdowns everyone was at home and could find time to listen to what was happening in the streets, the George Floyd video was on another level in terms of gruesomeness, a lot of people couldn't digest its contents. That nine-minute clip was too long for many people to complete watching.

The society has had enough of such bad behavior and could not take it anymore. This time around it wasn't only about the blacks, but all peoples of color in America felt the pain, they saw themselves in the eyes of this poor suffering man, a lot of white kids have black friends in their schools and workplaces, they therefore joined the protests as a way of protecting their friends from a potential murder by a crooked cop. The handling of the issue also contributed to the increase in the number of protesters, when they saw the officer involved being given a simple dismissal from his job, it angered them even more, they went ballistic with their screams. They waited for a short while as they watched the fellow being charged then given a lenient sentence. Now the protesters completely lost their cool, this was the final straw, it was like the animal in them had been let out to fully express its wild feelings. It was no surprise the protesters were infiltrated by hooligans who went about pillaging and destroying Property in the cities they went through.

The fact that protesters chose to go out into the streets at the height of the pandemic, a time when the whole world was tucked behind closed doors holding their breath as the Pandemic was consuming the lives of tens of thousands of people, proved how fed up they were & how terrible they felt. They all ignored the fact that they were putting their lives at risk by exposing themselves to a deadly virus of which very little was known about, they risked their personal safety and freedoms by fearlessly confronting antiriot police who were poured out onto the streets of America to stop them, yet they went ahead with their plans, they no longer feared getting arrested or be charged for causing civil unrest, their actions were a testament to the anger that was brewing from deep within, the incident provided an opportunity to release decades long worth of steam. They were simply unstoppable, what started with only a few people ended up being a crowd of millions walking the streets of America.

There have also been comparisons on the treatment of *BLM Protesters* and *January Capital building Riots*. Some experts are saying that the reason the law enforcement acted towards the BLM Protesters with a lot of brute force yet when a similar thing happens a year later, they stood by and just watched protesters invading the Capital Building, the very beating heart of United States government, they claim that all that behavior had to do with the skin color of the protesters, black protesters always face the full force of antiriot police, they are always tear-gassed, tazed, have fierce police dogs unleashed at them, thrown into police trucks, and sometimes brutally beaten by the antiriot police, however peaceful their protests may be, they are always handled very roughly, on the other hand white protesters face little consequences for their actions, people throw them flowers when they march along the streets as they shout their slogans, even when they cause damage to property and the Police are called on them, the cops hardly take any action, they simply standby and simply beg them not to hurt anyone.

Servitude-8-New global attention - the world is closely watching the Yankees Stadium

Since the start of the events that proceeded the passing of George Floyd, the whole world started looking at the US from a different lens, people are paying more attention, and getting curious with what is happening in America, many countries are now questioning the beliefs they had about America. It has always been taught that America is a place where many people of all races live together in peace and harmony with one another. countries are thinking of debunking it as a myth. Americans are now being questioned to the point where their own country's internal affairs risk being meddled with by outsiders. It is said that America is the most racially diverse country in the world. That you will find people from virtually every known nation, culture and religion in the world, but that diversity is not reflected in the highest of offices of the country. an almost all white congress and Wallstreet speaks volumes which is that we don't really have a representation of all peoples as the public is always taught.

The George Floyd incident opened a Pandora's box. The whole world is now paying attention, and with the help of modern-day technology, people are now digging up their sources a little bit deeper trying to find out what is going on in America. Some countries that are well known for having very serious human rights issues started lecturing America. It used to be the other way round, the US government has been giving good lectures to some world's dictatorships about the needs to strengthen the institutions that promote justice and equality in their countries as well as the preservation of Human rights. More and more horror stories are beginning to emerge in the endless American story. Does it have to be that every black man should be walking around everywhere with a hidden body camera? To prove his innocence every time he gets framed? A lot of BLM activists believe that modern technology has helped exposed a lot of social issues in the American society, most of them believe that the cameras haven't captured even the tip of the iceberg of the things they go through in their daily lives. There is still more of the story to tell." says the BLM Protesters. *"We are not trying to make white People look bad, we simply have grievances that need to be heard."* So, sit tight on the sofa and listen to us carefully.

In the wake of the Killings, the protesters who went to the streets were initially black then later joined by their white friends who were appalled by the video, to many white kids the images were a great shocker to them, a very chilling information that black kids knew all along. *"oh! so you are learning about that now?"* they say it to their white friends. The talks about these issues were a part and parcel of their daily coaching since childhood, they are taught to fear the white cop. Who has been made to appear more as a grim reaper than a guardian angel in the neighborhood.

I have also heard that dogs and cats get better treatment from white folks than what the blacks get from the same fellows. Dogs and cats have more rights than black people, they get mandatory medical or some kind of health checkup every other weekend, they eat nice food and have a warm shelter to protect them from the elements. In America when you kill a dog or a cat, you go to jail because you have violated **animal rights**, but if you kill a black man, you go free, no one is gonna bother you except for the family of that black guy, the black man has no rights, domestic pets are living a better and more enjoyable life than most black people, most of the things these animals enjoy the negroes can only dream of.

We also see a lot of white people share their beds with their pets and sometimes dangerous wildlife like lizards and snakes, they are very comfortable around these wild animals yet get spooked whenever they see a black guy in their exclusive white neighborhood, they often get anxious even when that Person is several hundred yards away.

Have also noticed that Black people in the USA are not called just Americans, they are always referred to as *"**AFRICAN** Americans"* or **BLACK** *Americans*, the word *African* is always overemphasized. To some of these white folks they are more of Africans than they are Americans and therefore cannot be just called Americans. They are not really Americans, "Only US citizens of *Caucasian Origin* should call themselves *real* Americans.

it's the Americans of European ancestry that call themselves just Americans but to other races they always put a name tag on them to indicate their place of origin, they call others, *"**AFRICAN** Americans, **ASIAN** Americans, **LATINOS** and **ARABS**. They always put a name tag to every other race that is in the USA except their own. They even look down upon Native Americans by calling them *"**INDIANS**"* to insinuate that they are not really Americans but some savages that came from the Indian Subcontinent to inhabit the Americas. *Why do you keep calling indigenous people Indians? Why do you keep referring to the native inhabitants of north America as Indians?* They are not at all Indians, and no time in history have they ever been Indians, in fact the term, *"**RED INDIAN**"* that has been used for centuries is such a demeaning and dehumanizing term.

It is high time now that the other races should start referring to the white folks as **EUROPEAN** Americans and not just Americans.

In a race argument, a black guy brings up a story of the suffering of the black slaves under their white masters, a white guy interjects angrily saying that slavery existed in the past and those responsible were long dead and gone, the current generation has nothing to do with that sad history. Then the black guy says " I am not just talking about our past suffering but our present subjugation as well. You see nothing much has changed then." Those white folks that tried to help the slaves free themselves paid dearly, there were a lot of white guys that were lynched alongside the blacks for the crime of trying to alleviate the suffering of the slaves, no one was ever free from these angry mobs, including a siting us president was not spared, even though Abraham Lincoln held nearly all the power in the country, he wasn't really in a safe place far away enough from the murderous racists.

Attempts to alleviate the suffering of the black community have continually been met with a lot of backlash from the society, there have been cases of young folks suing schools because they thought racial quotas caused them to miss positions in those schools even when they were fully qualified. They complained that poorly performing black students have forcefully been given admissions at the expense of other more qualified students just for the sake of filling a racial quota. There are companies who are complaining that they have been forced to hire less qualified staff to fill a racial quota, therefore leading to the underperformance of their company, these are bottlenecks the American society is still going through. they say you can't just make the society much better by throwing a bunch of folks into technical positions they are not even qualified for just because you pity their skin color, it only compounds the problem. The only positive result of this upheaval is that Black people are being appointed into high government offices right now simply because of the pressure from the BLM protesters.

Servitude-9-You gotta come clean

The only way Americans can overcome this menace is when they come clean, conduct a national dialogue about race and indigenous issues then come together as a family, otherwise if they do not properly address this matter, it would further escalate and threaten to tear the Nation Apart.

Racial Tensions are the sure thing that may destroy America from within, if people are no longer patriotic and more concerned about defending their own race then the nation loses its cohesive strength which will allow other foreign rivals to easily defeat it. Appeasement should be one if it's necessary, when there is no other way.

Some BLM Activists are saying, *"America is a nation that had many skeletons in her closet. She needs to confess her sins and seek forgiveness for her past wrongs,"* I discovered that black people in America were angry about so many things going on in their lives, they were not only angry about the bad apples in the police department, they said they had many grievances that needed to be addressed. The incident has reminded them of their past suffering, it made them feel the past centuries wounds and scars that are yet to heal being inflamed once more.

At the time of the Nuremberg trials, Truman traveled Europe lecturing former Nazi officials that they should be nice to people who look different from them, they should not have treated the Jews in the appalling way they did, the world was shocked by the discovery of the appalling number of people that were subjected to the gas chambers. The German SS on the other hand were flabbergasted to hear a sitting US president speaking out against racial discrimination. This was in the late forties remember, just a handful of years after World War 2. When he left behind a country segregated across racial lines and confidently drove across Europe lecturing Germans against the dangers of racial bias towards Jews. His words could not be further from the truth.

Servitude-10-Black Myths

There are a lot of Myths about black People that have been perpetuated by the Social economic status of black People over the years and also due to some degree of racial Prejudice in North America. Let us debunk a couple of these myths one by one.

1.Black don't hike or mountain Bike

There is an urban myth that black folks don't like going up onto the mountains simply because they are afraid of heights. Well, you don't have to be a genius to know that isn't true, there are two reasons why that is possible, first it's social-economic then second its life experiences. A vast majority of black people just like many other white Americans live from paycheck to paycheck. They don't have any spare cash or the luxury of time to go out on long excursions. Even when they go on excursions, it would be a short visit to the local national parks with their families, they prefer something that would take a single day, let's say a weekend getaway, then return home safely. If they had the money, then you would be seeing them spending entire weeks in the woods. It's rare to see a black American going out camping in the woods for weeks or months, simply because their bank account simply won't allow them. You rarely ever see a black person spending millions of dollars on an RV or something expensive to be used for staying out in the wild countryside. Any extra money earned is always put away for safe keeping to cushion the family against any hard times that may come in the future. Another issue is the danger that extreme sports exposes people to. since most black people already go through a life full of danger in their daily lives, they have learnt to be cautious and risk averse.

They don't like taking unnecessary risks especially ones that will put their lives into another set of dangers, why would you waste your time climbing rocks and mountains? For what reason is that? If you slip or fall and break your back, who would take care of your family when you are probably the sole breadwinner? A lot of black folks don't have adequate health insurance in their home states, they always get rejected by their local hospitals even for treatment of very minor ailments. Now picture this scenario, a black man decides to become an adrenaline junkie, he goes to the maintains and starts climbing rocks, let's then say there is an unfortunate avalanche accident that breaks his leg, he then comes home limping but no hospital wants to treat him because he has no proper health insurance. Everyone in his neighborhood starts calling him a fool. *"what were you thinking going up the mountains? Will climbing rocks take care of your young family."* they would torment him. Black folks are more sensitive to the dangers of outdoor excursions because they already experience them in their day today lives.

2.Black Can't Swim or surf

Another myth is that black folks can't swim because of their biological or some kind of genetic drawbacks. Some racist scientist theorized that black folks have extremely heavy bones that causes them to struggle staying afloat on water. Therefore, cannot compete against the white folks when swimming or surfing the waves. A sane person knows this is absolute rubbish. If you actually dig dip into American swimming cultures and water sports in general. You will find out that not until very recently, black folks didn't have access to swimming Pools. They couldn't build pools in their own backyards because of financial and state regulatory reasons, they weren't allowed access to public swimming pools for decades even after the civil rights movements of the sixties.

We all know that black folks are always present in the sports and athletics arenas, when America goes to the Olympics, it's they that are the country's flag bearers. They dominate the athletics, ball games such as football and basketball, gymnastics etc. this is because such fields of sports are free for all and allow anyone from any background to join. When many states started building basketball courts in almost every neighborhood in America some decades ago, a lot of black youth started experimenting with the game, some became very skilled and later became pro players, decades later the NBA is now dominated by black athletes. So are other sports that give equal opportunity for all. So let's put it simply that black folks weren't able to excel in swimming simply because of limited access to resources that facilitate this sport. It has nothing to do with having heavy bones. Build swimming pools in those ghettos and you will start seeing black kids swimming like fish in no time.

3.Black can't be good in science or math

Well, that is a preserve of the whites only and mostly Asians, they say that the reason most black kids end up failing schools is because they are dump and have nothing to do with their social economic status or the environment in which they are raised in. some racist folks even say that black kids like dropping out of schools when math and other sciences become too difficult for them. They abandon formal classes when it becomes too difficult for their brains to handle. There is an overwhelming information on the web that black schools are usually less funded and the kids always get low quality education, there is always very little interest from their local state officials to try and improve their academic situations.

There are many discussions on the web about black folks who made world changing inventions but could not get credit for their work because their masters took the responsibility of patenting the work. There are inventions made centuries ago by slaves yet no one acknowledged them simply because their masters took all the credit. Well, if black folks were dump in sciences, then they won't manage to conduct these incredible inventions.

In my primary school years, I used to read the life stories of doctor Ben Carson, I was interested in his experiences in his childhood and career, he talks about how much pain he felt in early school years when he was belittled by his teachers even though he was the best student in his class. He mentions an incident of how his racist white teacher berated other white kids for allowing themselves to be beaten by a black kid in academics. To her, black kids weren't supposed to perform well, at least not better than white kids. Such incidences are experiences that stuck with doctor Carson all his life. His career and life in general was full of odds stacked against him yet he persevered and made it to the finish line. He worked extra hard, harder than any other student in his class yet he still remained pinned down by the social dogmas. It wasn't only after he started performing miracles to his patients at john Hopkins that the society started paying him the respect and dignity he deserved.

4.Blacks are criminal by nature.

I don't know of any racial group in this world that doesn't have criminals among them, even though it may be negligible depending on the socio-economic situations of a community, for instance in affluent neighborhoods robbery may be very minimal, mostly because every resident in that community is surrounded by other rich neighbors, so who would think of going to steal a neighbor's Fridge when you spend an equivalent amount of money of the fridge price on fuel for your vehicle in just a single week. The other crimes that may be present in the wealthy neighborhoods could be homicides and others, people kill for other reasons that are not related to money. Homicides are present in all neighborhoods both the rich and poor. But when you are walking through a rundown ghetto community, you always keep your guard up, because you know very well at the back of your head that you can easily get mugged any minute. When you are walking across the streets alone, your heart is pumping so hard while your mind is a hundred percent alert, imagining a guy rushing towards you, grabbing your valuables either wallet or purse then making off with it. You can easily be attacked any moment by a complete stranger. There are some ignorant folk who wholeheartedly believe that the reason people from ghettos engage in crime especially robbery is simply because they are immoral by nature and lack human virtues, they are completely incapable of being virtuous in their lives, if you were to ask them, "*well if every adult person in this poor neighborhood had a well-paying job and all their kids went to good private schools, would there be crime as bad as it is right now?*" they say NO, it won't reach the level it is right now, because they will see no need to steal. " well, they are now beginning to learn, if you get these black guys out of the ghettos, then put in other races in their place, would the problem go away? " no, it won't" then what! You see how, you are quick to judge a particular community yet you are not willing to dig deeper into their history. You first need to be willing to walk in another person's shoes before you can start to judge them.

The so-called experts claim that the Indians in America have the best criminal record in the system, finding an Indian American robbing a bank is so rare it's like searching for a coin in a trash pit. This therefore concludes that Indians are morally upright people by nature. Well, if you go to their home country in India, you won't be saying that, with a country of more than a billion you can surely never miss some loose screws. Robbery with violence and other crimes are rampant in India just as they are in north America. The Indians that make it to north America are usually the good ones, most of them have lots of dreams and ambitions and once they land in America, they focus on the things that brought them into the country, they either go to Silicon Valley to build some cool tech gadgets or go into entrepreneurship programs to begin working on incredible startups, they are the working class who simply have no time for American bullshit.

There are certain situations that drive people to desperation. However morally upright you were raised, when the hunger pangs begin to bite, you will be forced to resort to desperate measurers, haven't you read in stories about the misery that befell the city of Jerusalem when the Roman Emperor Vespasian and his son Titus decided to lay a siege on the city, Jerusalem was the most morally upright city of its time, yet the inhabitants were not ready to experience what was about to come. The presence of a few rebels in the city caused the romans the cut off the entire supply chains of the city. Nothing was coming into the city for many months until when those dwelling inside ran out of food, many had no choice but to turn to the abominable act of cannibalism, they boiled their own children for food. They never imagined in their entire lives that one day they will end up behaving this way, yet they did. They were simply trying to survive; they didn't act that way because they were immoral. They were simply acting out of instincts.

In some exclusively white neighborhoods of America, black guys are really feared, some folks decide to teach their children that black guys are extremely dangerous and should be avoided as much as necessary. When a black man walks past white kids playing in their backyards, then as soon as the kids spot them, they ran away to their parents crying, "mummy mummy" their mother answers them, "what is it again? "There is a black man standing on our lawn, "you taught us to run away whenever we see a black man walking towards us. The mother then turns, she looked at the guy, and says to the kids, "no, never mind, it's just the pizza delivery man." But her face shows expression of embarrassment. Black folks say that there are places where you go and see people staring at you, even if they never say a word, their faces tell it all, some are frightened, others are shocked and some are trying to process what they have just seen, it's like they have seen a ghost, their body languages simply reads, "hey boy, you are in the wrong neighborhood, please get out of our faces."

I have heard black people say that they sometimes get double searched when going through an airport security in America. When you are the only black person in a room and something gets lost or stolen, you are always the first suspect. When charged with a crime, The black man is always guilty until proven innocent. It is sad that things have reached to this point where all black men have to walk around with their entire bodies strapped with cameras for first of all to protect them from rowdy citizens who might try to frame them, then secondly from the ***so-called bad apples in the law enforcement department*** that are always out there to get them.

Servitude-11-Black Success

There are few incidences in America where many black folks have had success which is in the Talent industry, especially the music and sports. *There is a saying in the hood that if you can't Sing or slam dunk, then you have no place in America.* For every black man in this neighborhood, if you don't have any kind of natural talent then you should forget about getting rich someday, no amount of hard work is gonna push you above the poverty line.

It is arguable that in America, to some degree your skin color does have an influence on the quality of life you are to lead from the moment you are born. It does not dictate one hundred percent how you are going to live but it does have an influence however small or large that may be.

Black Blues

Why are black folks so damn good at singing? Do you listen how sweet their blues and RNBs are?
Well for a long time now since the time of the plantations, they invented the blues to help them overcome the suffering they were going through under their cruel masters on the plantations. Later on it became part of their culture. In the 20th centuries it eventually became their source of revenue that could pull them out of poverty when white owned label companies started accepting black music. They stuck on it to this very day. Well, you know there is a lot of crap hip-hop music out there, there is also a lot of good black music out there

too. A significant proportion of all-time hit songs produced in north America are produced by black folks.

Looking at entertainment as a form of overcoming the stresses of slavery, the black slaves in Latin America joined the Carnivals. Now the world enjoys the carnivals from big Latin American countries like Brazil all thanks to the slaves' creative genius. It looks like the carnivals and the sweet soothing music are the only good things that came out of slavery. So sad a tale

Black Sports

It is evident how afro Americans are dominant in global sports and athletics. They have done a great job in representing their country to the world in the most positive way possible. For decades now Black athletes often formed a significant proportion of the Olympic teams and they always bring home lots of medals. The USA always makes it to the top three candidates in terms of total number of medals collected, thanks to a significant share contributed by black athletes. When a black man is done running the Olympic track, he is back home in America running away from trouble, running from racist hooligans, local thugs and crooked cops, the black man is always running for his life back at home, so when you take them to international competitions, they laugh at other athletes saying, "look, we have been running all our lives, what makes you think you can be like us?"

Servitude-12-Greatest Black Americans

Which of these three black men is greatest? Is it Barrack Obama or George Floyd, Malcolm X, or Martin Luther King Jr? Which one has impacted most people in a positive way? If you are to rank these fellows in a descending order of greatness who is going to come last?

Most of you would go for the Kenyan Son, Obama even though he has achieved very great & seemingly impossible tasks, many people feel that since he didn't suffer much, he spent his professional life in the luxurious oval office while the others were being brutalized on the streets of America. Yeah, that's right, many would argue, Obama is far Lesser than Malcolm X, Martin Luther King JR and George Floyd, these guys paid the ultimate price for their cause, which is of course their own lives.

Obama is now enjoying his comfortable retirement, he has done a lot to change Americans perspectives about having a black leader, Americans can now elect any person into the oval office irrespective of their skin color, but Obama didn't pay the ultimate price of his political moves, we can therefore say that he is lesser than George Floyd, Malcolm X and Martin Luther King Junior.

Servitude-13-The Work of Other Black Activists

Other Black Activist Like Malcolm X. Isaiah Mohamed and Martin Luther King did an incredible Job to improve the situation of the Black community in America. A couple of black activists turned away from Christianity because of the racism in the church, People like martin Luther king junior, however used the same Bible to fight oppression of the afro American community and got more success than any other black activists of his time. The sane white folks realized that the racists pastors were doing an incredible damage to the church by turning many people of color away from Christ. To them, these rowdy ministers were the epitome of the antichrist that was foretold ages ago that he will turn many believers away from Jesus. There is a good reason why a lot of afro Americans call **Christianity a white man's religion**, there is a good reason why some of them are so rebellious and do not wish to cooperate with any white folks, for this religion called Christianity was used to enslave their ancestors, and its being used now to intimidate and humiliate them.

The Infamous KKK used a burning cross as their logo symbol, they wore their Christian crosses as they went about ravaging black communities, they kept on pillaging neighborhoods, burning homes and murdering black folks they came across. It was such a horrific site to see a group of rowdy white folks dressed in white garments, and carrying burning crosses searching their neighborhoods for victims. When the *"cross"* a sacred Christian symbol is used to lynch innocent people, it by no doubt does incredible damage to the church especially in the eyes of the black community, The Klansmen tainted the holy image of the cross.

Another infamous group that used images of Christianity to accomplish great evil were the German Nazis, The Swastika is a simple shape of a twisted cross, yes you heard me right. "the Nazis took a symbol that is adorned by all Christendom and twisted its edges to be used for their own wicked deeds. They went around Europe and north Africa committing acts of genocide. If they weren't defeated in World War 2 by an alliance of world superpowers, they would have probably wiped out a half of the world's population.

Servitude-14-MJ Music

Come on Let's be serious, whatever made Michael Jackson Change his skin color, nobody really knows for sure, not unless he himself came forth to explain himself to the world, nobody is ever going to understand Many BLK folks would like to argue that it was the pressure he had from the industry that forced him to undertake that uncouthly procedure. Most of the fans of the genre were YT, and it was they who had the resources to fund his music careers by attending his concerts.

They also say that it's the pressure from these YT Fans that forces many would be celebrities to bleach their skin so that they can appeal to their audience, dark skin used to be greatly frowned upon in the entertainment industry, be it movies, music, fashion modeling, magazines, journalism or whatever, the darker your skin was the harder it was to get accepted by the agency.

There was a story of a young female intern who got rejected by a major news agency, despite all her academic qualifications they rejected her application to become a news anchor saying that she was *"too dark"*, and her face would therefore not make a good representation of the company.

Servitude-15-Bob Marley's Movements

Another popular musician that criticized the institutions of modern-day slavery and ending up dying mysteriously is none other than the Jamaican Legend Bob Marley. His death is very mysterious as well as very controversial, he passed on at a prime young age of 36 years in a Miami hospital. Millions of people across the world truly loved his songs, he left his legacy in the hearts and minds of millions of people. Many of his fans still believe that his death was very suspicious, it wasn't at all natural. Or anything to do with a prolonged illness. They believe he was simply eliminated.

His lyrics were filled with songs that condemned the institution of slavery in America. The likes of his song like *"Buffalo Soldier"* highlighted the plight of black soldiers in the American Indian wars and the American civil wars, he praises their courage and gallantry, the fact that they were greatly despised in the country they were fighting and dying for was something that touched bob Marley's heart. He sang other songs like *"One Love. One Heart."* that inspired peoples of different racial backgrounds to live in harmony with one another. His songs were romantic as well as political, so they didn't do well especially with some politicians living in North America.

There are claims all over the internet of people claiming to be responsible for bob Marley's death, a guy spoke a few years ago saying that he was directly involved in bob Marley's killing. He claimed that he was a former CIA covert operative who was sent to finish off Mr. Marley. His songs which were becoming very popular in many black majority countries, were against the US foreign policy at the time, it was at the height of the cold war and the US government was very nervous, they didn't want to see another Caribbean fellow inspire an anti-American uprising in the Caribbean, in America's backyard, if they let that happen, the movements could spread to the whole of central and South America, and the rest of the world as well, this would be disastrous for the US Federal states, they didn't want to have a repeat of the Cuban uprising that led to the coming of Fidel Castro to power at America's doorstep. Castro had created so many problems for America already, they didn't want another Caribbean fool to add salt to injury, so they sent me to finish him off," says the fellow, Fidel Castro as the US experts put it was a thorn in the side of the Us Federal Government it was too risky to let another fellow sway the masses with his crazy doctrines.

Bob Marley didn't simply sing about love, cohesion and intermingling of people from different races, he directly appealed to African countries to unite and work together under a common brotherhood. He asked African governments to unite under one flag. So that they become stronger and more prosperous together, words that the superpowers of the world dreaded at the time. And when you look at Reggae culture itself, it is adorned with the colors of the Ethiopian flag, Rastafarianism is some kind of religion that is inspired by past victories of the modern-day nation state of Ethiopia. Ethiopia has an incredible history. Alongside Liberia they are the only African countries that have never been colonized by European powers in the nineteenth century, when the Italians marched down from Rome to the horn of Africa to subjugate its inhabitants, they found the Ethiopians ready and waiting for them, with a modern standard army with the latest lethal weapons, the Ethiopians were more than a match for the Italians.

They gave them a beating that they would never forget. The Ethiopians sent the Italians running to their motherland. The defeat of Italy, a major European power at the time shocked the entire continent of Europe, the Europeans that sent expeditions to Africa detoured Ethiopia as a result of this victory. They avoided the country as much as they can so that they can avoid unnecessary losses that may be inflicted on them by the Ethiopian army, they instead chose to journey onwards to the eastern parts, the so-called horn of Africa where they hoped for easy prey, they dreamt of finding primitive tribes that fight only with bows and arrows so that they can mow them down with their rifles and machine guns. For their bravery and determination to protect themselves, Ethiopia remained uncolonized by a European power.

Some European countries criticized Italy for their failure to beat the Ethiopian army, especially war hardened nations like Britain and France could have brought more reinforcements to recapture the country. Italy however was a relatively weak nation at the time according to European standards.
You remember the time when *The Mahdi* destroyed an entire British occupational force in Sudan. Well, the British got pissed off by it and later sent in reinforcements to avenge the death of its dear troops, they eventually defeated the Mahdi and his Sudanese tribesmen at *the battle of Omdurman*. Some scholars now argue that if it were either British or the French that had been defeated by Ethiopian forces, they probably would have sent reinforcements to wear down the Ethiopian army and eventually capture the country.

Bob Marley and his Rastafarian band truly adored the former Ethiopian leader *"emperor Selassie,"* they saw him as a true leader, a symbol of victory against western imperialism. A warrior that protected his people from potential enslavement by a European Power. In his songs he calls him, *Lion of Judah, Mighty Zion, Iron Lion"* and many more wonderful things. Such words were surely to get Marley into trouble for sure, they created for him quiet a lot of enemies. They are probably the lyrics that got him killed. Many Africans, afro Americans and afro Caribbean's strongly believe that Bob Marley was skillfully murdered by a global syndicate of CIA Operatives to silence him, even though they don't have any strong evidence to back up their claims they still believe it to be so. During his entire music career, Bob Marley remained a geopolitical activists armed only with a guitar and microphone fighting for global influence. His death shot him into greater fame and made reggae music known all over the world.

Servitude-16-Mohamed Ali's Conversion

Mohamed Ali's conversion could be associated with the racism he faced in America while growing up, even though he was a national hero and represented the country in several international events, he was shocked to discover that when he returned home, he was treated just like another stray dog by white Americans. When he was denied service by a waiter in a white only restaurant, he went ballistic, and swore to fight racism to the bitter end. His refusal to be forcefully drafted for the Vietnam war was another tumultuous episode in his life, it nearly ruined his career when he refused to go to Vietnam to fight an enemy he doesn't know while at home in America he was constantly taunted by an enemy he was familiar with. During his time, going to Vietnam was a choice for white kids but the black ones had no choice, they had to make themselves available when called upon.

Mohamed Ali constantly spoke about how the slave owners used every tool in their possession to keep the black man tied in shackles, they used everything including religion to oppress him, in some places verses of the bible that spoke out against the mistreatment of slaves were not read in churches or even removed entirely from the scriptures. He was surprised to discover that there were racist Pastors in the country who twisted verses of the bible to suit their own racist ideology. These are some of the things that made Ali hate going to church and gave him thoughts of trying a different religion that may bring peace and comfort to his heart. His friends and family were against his conversion but it was already too late. Ali had already made up his mind. Everything about his life to that point disgusted him. Even his own birth name had a racist connotation. He was born "Cassius Clay", which he thought as derogative, demeaning, when you give your fellow human being the name "Clay" you are insinuating that he is a worthless fellow, that he is no better than the dirt of the earth that people walk on. The word **clay** is a synonym for **dirt** and that doesn't sound good, especially to the ears of people like Mohamed Ali. He converted to Islam as a way of pretesting the oppressive institution of white Christianity.

To quote some of his interviews Ali Says, "
"I ask my mother, how come everything is white? Why is Jesus white with blonde hair and blue eyes? Why is the lord's supper all white men? Mary and Angels are white, …..even Tarzan the king of the jungles of Africa is white…..I

always wondered why miss America was always white, and miss world was always white and miss universe was always white... The angels' cake was white cake while the devil's cake was the chocolate cake.... And the president lives in the white house... Santa Claus was white and everything bad was black, the little ugly duckling was a black duck, and the black cat was the bad luck, and if I threaten you, I am gonna blackmail you, why can't they say whitemail?... this is when I knew something was wrong."

The despicable act of some racist pastors using the bible to condemn black skin caused a lot of black people to leave those churches to built their own. Those slanderous ministers were saying that black people were that way because they were cursed long ago. It's that curse from God many millennia ago that caused their skin to turn black. This was so unbearable for the black community that many of them considered atheism. They kept twisting the scriptures all the time. It led to the invention of terms like **black Jesus** among the Afro American community. To them God is supreme being creator of all humans and not the racist fanatic that some of those pastors try to portray him to be like.

Servitude-17-Comments that got 2PAC Killed

Its common knowledge that the death of The Legendary activists Malcolm X had something to do with some character in the Law Enforcement. Both Malcolm X and

MLK died from the bullets of some rogue elements within the Federal Bureau, the FBI Now is so ashamed of itself that they won't admit to the wrongs of their actions.

Many Afro Americans believe that it was the comments he made about US Foreign Policy that got him shot. He heavily criticized the US government for donating billions of dollars to help other countries while many poor people in the US who were disproportionately African Americans were dying of cold and hunger in the streets of America, so the deep state decided to finish him off and made it look like another incident of gang violence going off in the streets of America. "He looked like a gangster, he walked like a gangster, he talked like a gangster, he sang like a gangster, he was completely into gangster lifestyle, if we knock him off now, people are gonna think that it was his lifestyle that got him and no one else to blame. People are never gonna believe otherwise.
The US legal apparatus has the technology and resources to catch even the most sophisticated of all criminals.

They are even able to trace criminals that have fled to other countries and have them extradited back to the US. The law is always determined to get justice for everyone even those that are not well known, for a very famous persons case such as 2pac to go cold is a sure sign that some higher power is involved, that's why you will never know the real truth. People wonder why there are no living witnesses to the brazen crime that happened in an open street. Some folks in the black community said that 2pac has won the hearts of millions of Americans including the white folks, white kids exalted him as though he was some kind of deity, there could be elements of the Klan's men who weren't happy with the fact that their own daughters are flocking to his concerts to dance to his rap songs, to hug him and kiss him, they were tormented by the thoughts of rumors that 2Pac and his other black thugs were taking advantage of their daughters behind the scenes at the backstage, they thought they had to finish him off before things got worse.

Servitude-18-The Promises of a Black President

Winning the race to the white house by Barrack Obama in 2008 is probably the most promising times of American presidency. Americans were mesmerized by this youthful fellow who had some ancestry from the ends of the world. His mother had some Irish roots while his father was of Kenyan ancestry. When Obama won the elections, many people's hopes were raised. They said to one another, *"if a black man with African roots can become a president in America, what then is not possible in this world? anyone can achieve anything they want to, right?"* People truly believed that America and the rest of the world are going to change for the better. If that is the case. I was part of a small group of students who created a party in our college to celebrate Obama's victory. Black Americans too were happy just like everyone else, they saw the trials of their lives all coming to an end, finally they were beginning to see the light at the end of the tunnel. Obama's victory in 2008 elections raised a lot of hopes for many black youths in America as well as the millions of young folks back on the continent, nearly all African countries celebrated his victory, they were relieved to finally see their own son about to step into the highest office in the world.

He was about to become the world's most powerful and influential man, and he was*(so they thought)* gonna use that office to help many Africans. They hoped he was going to help bring jobs to millions of jobless Africans, put an end to the destructive civil wars on the continent and reduce the suffering of the negro nations. All over the world, from the Caribbean to Latin America, from Asia to the middle east, from Africa to Oceania, Obama's election victory was received with great optimism. Compared to other leaders that came before him, he was a relatively young man whose prime face was a symbol of freshness and vitality. "this young man is going to do great things for America and the world" people said. The spirits were high in the African American communities as well as on the African continent, and the black majority Caribbean group of nations.

It was in his father's home country of Kenya that the celebrations reached their Zenith, Kenyans were overjoyed to watch their son walk into the white house, the so called *" Highest office in the world"* people couldn't stop dancing for days and weeks, especially in his grandmother's village of *Kogelo in Western Kenya*, celebrations went on for months. His grandmother, friends, family and neighbors were overjoyed. They just couldn't stop singing.

Well with all these hopes, why did many people end up disappointed? They did not see the fruition of the things that they hoped Obama will deliver to them, the afro Americans were the least critical of him because they knew clearly how the US system of government worked. But many Africans were pissed off, they couldn't understand what was happening, *" why is Obama refusing to help us"* the Africans ask themselves, *" moreover, why is he refusing to help his own people in America, the black guys that are suffering in the very country he runs, he should at least have helped release some of those poor black guys from prison"* they enquire. People asked, *"why didn't Obama help Africans? Or why didn't he do anything to alleviate the suffering of blacks in America when he was in office?"*

This is not a simple question to answer, and for those who don't know, The united States of America is run by institutions that are several centuries old, they are not controlled from the office of the president, and no sitting president in America irrespective of his skin color, has the power to release a convicted man from prison without constitutional process, a US president can't simply visit a correctional facility and then give orders to the prison guards to release the prisoners, that can never happen in this part of the world. America has some of the strongest institutions in the world, the nation works like a well-oiled machine, even if you have the most illiterate and ignorant president in office, the institutions can run the country smoothly even in the most difficult of times.

The institutions are so powerful that they can run the country in the full absence of the president for months and years without risking any kind of civil unrest. ***America's civil war of mid 1800s*** was the first and the last, even though millions of Americans own firearms, the citizens would never go to war with one another again over political differences, the American people are too smart for that now, they can never tear their country apart because of bipartisan politics, and the whole world knows that.

Elected presidents are shocked the moment they get into the oval office, when they finally discover how much little power they actually have. Ninety percent of America's government power is owned by the institutions, which then give the remaining ten percent to the president so as to calm him down in his oval office, to make him believe that his bid for presidency and all the time, energy and resources spent on the campaigns was not all in vain. Obama found out about this the hard way, and so did Donald trump. They discovered that the legal limitations would not allow them to fulfil all their campaign promises. And every other American president that comes after Biden, will have to deal with the heavy chains put on his arms and feet by America's institutions.
In the last year of Obama's presidency, he visited Kenya the birthplace of his father, he gave the locals a clue of why he didn't visit the country of his beloved

grandmother early on in in his presidency, he said that he would have received a lot of backlash back in America had he visited Kenya immediately after becoming president, so he had a good reason to detour the world first before setting is foot at home, he knew that he had a lot of haters, and didn't want to give them a good reason to attack him.

Back in America his *Americanness* or should I say US citizenship was already being questioned. There were people in the opposition who were already saying that Obama was not really an American but a Kenyan born African. He was pushed so hard to the point where he had to release his birth certificate to prove that was born in America. Earlier during his campaigns, Obama used his African roots to inspire millions of Americans to vote for him, unfortunately those same roots were being used against him when he entered the oval office, whenever he tried to do something that would help the African continent, he would immediately get attacked by the opposition as well as members of his own party. *"So you are an African now, you are not really an American, are you?"* They asked him.

During Obama's presidency whenever African Americans complained about racism, they would be told, *"well you have a black president now, what else do you want?"* you know having a black president in oval offices doesn't necessarily stop racism, it doesn't automatically change the structures that have been put in place for many centuries, experts believe that it may take several more centuries for the emancipation of the black man to become complete. Remember that after Abraham Lincoln abolished slavery, the lives of the slaves didn't improve immediately, the federal government didn't have the full power to reinforce the laws in all American communities, in fact there were cities and towns that clung onto their slaves and refused to let them go. They were used to having a very easy life that was built by slave labor and didn't want to lose even a single fraction of that, slavery therefore went on for several more decades, it only stopped when it became old fashioned at the dawn of the twentieth century.

There are cases of white Americans that kept slaves in their homes even as recently as after World War two. Way into the late fifties and sixties. And they were so secretive about it that they thought they would never be found.
When the Obamas entered office in 2009, they discovered some very sensitive documents that had been hidden away in the archives for centuries, these documents gave the world enough information, a solid proof that the white house building itself, a symbol of American pride and prosperity was built with the help of black slaves. The white guys did the simple drawings then after that sat back to toss champagne while the black guys did all the difficult work of lifting bricks and mortar, mixing concrete and carrying super heavy logs. There is possibility that a lot of US government buildings were done by the hands of the black slaves, it's just that the records were either unfortunately lost, secretly hidden, or deliberately

destroyed by the officials to wipe out the important role played by black guys in building America. Even though there could have been many that worked and died on the construction sites, none of them got a single credit for the work they did for America's future prosperity.

Conclusion

Let us be clear here, I am not an expert is slavery or slave history, most of the content above is just public opinion that I have derived from the conversions that exploded on the internet after the Gorge Floyd incident in May 2020. Well, I am not an expert on this topic. This article is just touching on things that have already been touched by others. If you have any valuable information on this subject, please put it in the reviews section. I shall be glad to look at it. If you have a topic that you would like to educate me on this subject you can always drop me an inbox on my website... *"wordstoelate.com"*

END OF SERVITUDE.

##

Final Clause

We have come to the end of our conversation, looking forward to connecting to you soon. We shall have more to discuss.

Please leave your thoughts & queries about this text in the reviews section, if you have something that needs further elaboration or have got some burning question, you can always text me and I shall be more than happy to respond appropriately.

Write to me,
DodeSescri@gmail.com

**NB*
Make sure you have the latest version of this text, you should check for newer versions at your favourite stores in order to get instant access to free content updates.

Thank you for your time.

Footnotes.

My most used/favourite stylistic features
- Sharp contrast
- Heavy metaphor
- Extravagant exaggeration.

----------------HIJK----------------------------
The information provided above may not be certain

----------------HIJK----------------------------

"Hold on sir/madam, you want to say something, please
hold back your words, I know what you want to say, to
complement on it upfront, you may be right, but for now
please let billy sell his pancakes to the princess"

The reference to masculine or feminine characters In the
above stories is not a biased motive to discriminate
against any gender, it's just for the purposes of description,
the authors repeated use of words such as
he/him/man/king are just for the purposes of enchanting
the narrative, if you feel offended by them then feel free to
replace them with whatever words you choose as you read
along, these pronouns are NOT put in place to intimidate,
you can also contact the author directly and specify which
part should changes be made to and to what particular
effect, the author respects all readers and will not
misrepresent members of any class, age, status or gender.
All readers are precious.

I am trying to avoid the inconvenience of having to jump
from one side of the group to another as it easily puts the
readers off, jumping from side to side, back and forth,
here and there is really irritating, take for instance it's
better to say, "the king came out of his castle, called the
knights and asked him to take him out on a ride through

the royal forests and left his son in charge of the castle,"
than to say, "the king/queen came out of his/her castle,
called the knight/knightess and asked him/her to take
him/her out on a ride through the royal forest and left
his/her son/daughter in charge of the castle"

Textual homogeneity- some aspects of the words, phrases
and stories share lots of similarities with one another, the
keen reader who repeatedly crosscheck between different
tittles will definitely notice this trend, if characters are
portrayed in such a sluggish manner that makes the text
boring to the reader, then reader please remember to
inform the author as soon as possible.

Cover image: An African American slave together with a
native American offering services to a cowboy, theme by
the Author.